Samsung Galaxy A15 5G User manual For Beginners and Seniors

A comprehensive User Guide For Beginners and Seniors to explore the multifaceted capabilities of the Samsung Galaxy A15 5G Device like a pro.

Precious Livestone

2

Table of Contents

INTRODUCTION

Discover the interactive and informative User Guide for the Samsung Galaxy A15 5G Device, a resource meticulously crafted to enhance your device experience. Irrespective of your level of knowledge in mobile technology, this crucial tool empowers you with the necessary knowledge and skills to effortlessly navigate your device. Immerse yourself in this all-encompassing guide to unlock the full potential of the Samsung Galaxy A15 5G Device, unveiling a wealth of invaluable insights and techniques.

Various situations and potential remedies for device overheating

Should the device encounter a rise in temperature while the battery is being charged,

While the device is being charged, it is important to note that both the charger and the device itself have the potential to produce heat. It is not uncommon for the device to feel warmer to the touch when utilizing wireless charging or fast charging methods. It is crucial to understand that this increase in temperature is well within the device's normal operating parameters and will not have any adverse effects on its performance or lifespan. Nevertheless, it is worth mentioning that if the battery temperature reaches excessively high levels, it may result in a decrease in charging speed or even cause the charger to stop charging overall.

Once the device starts to generate heat, just do the following actions:

- In order to initiate the charging procedure again, disconnect the charger from the device and make sure to close all applications. It is important to let the device cool down before reattaching the charger.

- If the minor component of the device becomes excessively heated, it could be attributed to a defective USB cable. To rectify this problem, all you need to do is substitute the damaged USB cable with a completely new one that has received official endorsement from Samsung.

- In order to maintain the optimal performance of the wireless charger, it is crucial to refrain from placing any foreign objects, such as metal items, magnets, or magnetic stripe cards, between the charger and the device.

- Erase all unnecessary files or unused applications.

- Reduce screen brightness.

Chapter One
Charge device battery

Before using your battery for the first time, make sure it is fully charged. Additionally, if you haven't used your battery for an extended period, it is advisable to charge it.

To ensure your safety and the optimal functioning of your device, it is imperative to exclusively utilize Samsung-approved batteries, cables specifically designed for your gadget, and chargers. The use of incompatible chargers, batteries, or cables poses a significant risk of causing severe harm to both you and your device.

- Improperly connecting your charger to your device can cause significant harm. It's important to note that any damage caused by misuse is not covered under the warranty.

- To ensure the safety of your device, it is imperative to exclusively utilize the USB Type-C cables that were originally provided with your device. The use of a Micro USB cord can potentially result in damage to your device.

- To conserve energy, it is important to unplug your charger when it is not in use. Since the charger does not have a power switch, it is necessary to disconnect it from the electrical outlet whenever it is not being utilized to avoid wasting power. While charging, it is recommended to keep the charger close to the electrical outlet for easy access.

Charging via a wired connection

In order to replenish the battery of your device, simply insert the USB cable into the versatile jack and connect it to the USB power adapter. Once the charging process is complete, disconnect the charger from your smartphone.

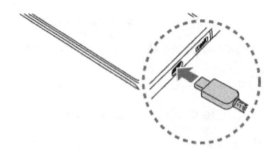

Fast charge your device

To access your desired feature, navigate to the Settings application, click on Battery & device care, select→ Battery→, then tap on More battery's setting and enable it.

- To take advantage of your fast charging capability, it is recommended to use a battery charger that is compatible with Adaptive fast charging.

Charging your battery becomes even more efficient when your device or its screen is turned off.

Reduce the consumption of your battery

Your device offers a variety of options that can assist you in preserving your battery life.

- To optimize the performance of your device, take advantage of the device care feature available to you.

- When your device is not in use, simply press the side key to power off the screen.

- Activate the power-saving mode.

- Ensure that any applications that are not in use are properly closed down.

- Make sure to disable your Bluetooth when it is not in use.

- Disable the automatic synchronization feature for applications that necessitate being in sync.

- Reduce the length of time your backlight remains on.

- Diminish the intensity of your screen's brightness.

Guidelines and precautions for battery charging

- If your device's battery is completely depleted, it cannot be immediately turned on once you connect the charger. It is recommended to wait a few minutes for a discharged battery to charge before using your device.

- If you engage in network applications, utilize apps that necessitate connectivity to another device, or have multiple applications open simultaneously, your battery will deplete quickly. To avoid power loss during data transfers, it is advisable to use these applications only when your battery is fully charged.

- If you use a power source other than a charger (such as a computer), charging may be slower because less current flows.

- Your device can be used while charging; however, it may take longer for the battery to fully charge.

- If your device charges from an irregular power source, your touch screen may not work. In this case, disconnect the charger from the device.

- The smartphone and charger may become hot during charging. This is a typical phenomenon and does not affect the functionality or lifespan of the device. If the battery gets hotter than normal, the charger may stop charging.

- If you charge the multifunctional outlet when it is wet, the device may be damaged.

Before you change your device, please ensure the multifunction jack is dry completely.

- If charging does not work properly, take your device and charger to an authorized Samsung service center.

SIM/USIM card (Nano SIM card)

Insert the SIM or USIM card you received from your mobile operator.

If you wish to use two different phone numbers/service providers on one device, you can enter 2 SIM or USIM cards. In some regions, inserting two different SIM cards into your device may result in slower data transfer speeds than inserting one SIM card.

Depending on your provider, some services that require an internet connection may not be available.

Install SIM/USIM card

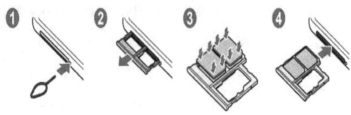

1 Insert the ejection pin into the opening on the side to release the compartment.

2 Carefully remove the tray from the trial slot.

3 Place the SIM/USIM card into the tray with the gold contacts facing down, and then gently push the SIM/USIM card into the tray to protect it.

4 Replace the tray into the tray slot.

- Only use nano SIM cards.

- Please be careful not to lose or use your SIM/USIM card without authorization. Samsung is not responsible for any loss or inconvenience caused by a lost or stolen card.

- Be right sure that the ejector pin is upright to the hole. Otherwise, your device may be damaged

- Your SIM card may become detached or fall out of the tray if it is not inserted securely.

- If the tray is placed in the device when it is wet, your device may be damaged. Make sure your pallets are always dry.

- To prevent liquid from entering your device, make sure the tray is fully inserted into the tray slot.

SIM card management

Open the Settings app and tap Connect → select SIM Manager.

- SIM card: Activate your SIM card for use and personalize your SIM card settings.

- Preferred SIM card: When two SIM cards are active, you can choose which SIM card to use for certain features, such as voice calls.

- Automatic data switching: If the SIM card selected by your device cannot establish a network connection, configure it to use another SIM card for data service.

- More SIM settings: Customize call settings to suit your preferences.

The memory card (microSD card)

Install your memory card

Your device's memory card capacity may vary by model. Depending on the manufacturer and type of memory card, some memory cards may not work with your device. For information about your device's maximum memory card capacity, visit the Samsung website.

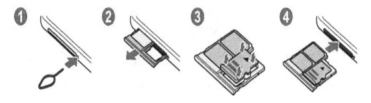

1 Input the ejection pin into the opening on the side to release the compartment.

2 Carefully remove the tray from the trial slot.

3 Place the SIM/USIM card into the tray with the gold contacts facing down, and then gently push the SIM/USIM card into the tray to protect it.

4 Replace the tray into the tray slot.

- Your device may not be fully compatible with all memory cards. Using an incompatible card may corrupt the data stored on the memory card or damage the device itself.

- Carefully insert the memory card, correct side up.

- Make sure the ejector pin is perpendicular to the opening. Otherwise, your device may be damaged.

- Your cellular connection will be turned off every time you remove the tray from your smartphone.

- Your memory card may become detached or fall out of the card slot if it is not inserted securely.

- If the tray is placed in the device when it is wet, your device may be damaged. Make sure your pallets are always dry.

- Insert the tablet fully into the compartment to prevent liquids from entering your device.

- The device is compatible with the FAT and exFAT file systems of memory cards. If you insert a card that is formatted with a different file system, your device will prompt you to reformat your card or may not recognize the card at all. Please make sure your memory card is formatted before you start using is. If your device has problems formatting or recognizing the memory card, please contact a Samsung service center or the memory card manufacturer.

- If you delete data frequently, your memory card will shorten its lifespan.

- When you insert a memory card into your device, the memory card's folder will appear under My Files → and then within the SD Card folder.

Remove your memory card

Before removing the memory card, you should remove it first for safer removal.

1 Open the Settings app and tap Battery & Device Care → select Storage.

2 To view the SD card page, swipe left.

3 Then click ⋮ → Uninstall.

Never remove external storage devices, such as memory cards or USB drives, while or after your device is accessing or transferring data. This puts you at risk of data corruption or loss as well as damage to external storage/devices. Samsung is not responsible for any damage (including data loss) caused by improper use of external storage devices.

Format your memory card

Your device may not work with a memory card formatted with a computer. Carefully format the memory card in the smartphone.

1 Open the Settings app and tap Battery & Device Care → and select Storage.

2 To view the SD card page, swipe left.

3 Then click ⋮ → Format.

Don't forget to back up all important information on your memory card before formatting. Data loss due to user action is not covered by the manufacturer's warranty.

Chapter Two
Turn your device on and off

Follow all warnings and instructions from authorized officials in locations where the use of wireless devices is prohibited, such as: B. In hospitals and on aircraft.

Turn on your device

To turn on the device, quickly press and hold the side button.

Turn off your device

1 To turn off the device, you should press and hold the side button. You can also open the notification panel, swipe down, and click on ⏻.

2 Then click Power off.

To reboot your device, click Restart.

Force restart

To restart your smartphone if it is frozen or unresponsive, you should press and hold the side button and the volume down button simultaneously for more than seven seconds.

Emergency mode

To save battery, you can put your device into emergency mode. Some apps and features will be limited. When you're in emergency mode, you can make emergency calls, tell people your current location, sound emergency alerts, and more. To activate emergency mode, you should press and hold the side button and then tap emergency mode. Alternatively, you can swipe down to show the notification panel and click the ⏻ → Emergency mode.

To turn off emergency mode, click the ⋮ →, then tap "Turn off emergency mode."

The remaining time before the battery is exhausted is indicated by the remaining usage time. Remaining usage time may vary based on your device settings and operating conditions.

Chapter Three
The initial settings

Follow the on-screen instructions to properly set up your mobile device when you first turn it on or after performing a data reset.

During the initial setup process, it is possible that you will encounter difficulties configuring specific device features if you do not have a WiFi connection established.

Fingerprint recognition

In order for the fingerprint recognition to function properly, it is necessary to input and save your fingerprint information on your device.

- The presence of this feature may differ depending on the specific model or service provider.

- Device security is significantly enhanced through the utilization of fingerprint recognition, which takes advantage of the unique characteristics present in each individual's fingerprint. The likelihood of the fingerprint sensor mistakenly identifying two distinct fingerprints as the same is exceedingly low. However, in rare cases where two fingerprints bear a striking resemblance to each other, the sensor may inadvertently classify them as identical.

- Ensure that the screen protector you choose allows you to utilize the on-screen fingerprint sensor without any hindrance.

- If you lock the screen with your fingerprint, you will not be able to use your fingerprint to unlock the screen when you turn on your device for the first time. You must enter a PIN, password, or the pattern you selected when registering your fingerprint to unlock the screen before you can use the device. Make sure you haven't forgotten your PIN, password and pattern.

- If your fingerprint is not recognized, use the PIN, password, or pattern you set when you registered your fingerprint to unlock your device. Register your fingerprints electronically. If you forget your PIN, pattern or password and do not reset your device, you will no longer be able to use your device. Any data loss or issues caused by incorrectly entering the unlock code are not Samsung's fault.

- If you use the less secure "Swipe" or "None" screen lock methods, all of your biometric information will be deleted. If you want to use biometric data in apps or other services, you will need to re-register.

To enhance the accuracy of fingerprint identification

If you were to scan your fingerprints on your device, the functionality of this feature could be affected by the following factors.

- In the event that your fingerprints are marked by wrinkles or scars, there is a possibility that your device may encounter difficulty in recognizing them.
- Your device may not be able to recognize fingerprints from small or tiny fingers.

33

- To improve the accuracy of recognition, it is recommended to register the fingerprints of the hand you most commonly use to operate your device.

- The recognition fingerprint sensor on your device is conveniently located at the center of the bottom of your screen. It is important to ensure that no objects, such as keys, coins, pens, or necklaces, come into contact with or cause any harm to the fingerprint recognition sensor or your screen protector.

- Ensure that both your fingers and the area where the fingerprint recognition sensors are situated, which is located in the bottom center of your screen, are dry and clean.

- If you use your fingertips or bend your finger, there is a possibility that your device will not recognize your fingerprints. It is recommended to press on your screen firmly so that your fingertip covers the entire fingerprint recognition area. For better recognition performance, please register your fingerprints using the hand that you primarily use to perform tasks on the device.

Enrolling your fingerprints onto your device

1. To access your Settings, simply open the application and navigate to the Biometrics & security section, where you can then choose the option for Fingerprints.

2. After carefully reading the directions displayed on your screen, proceed by tapping the "Continue" button.

3. Next, you have the option to choose and apply any style of screen lock that suits your preferences.

4. To activate fingerprint recognition, place your finger on the sensor. If your device detects your fingerprint, simply lift your finger and reposition it on the sensor.

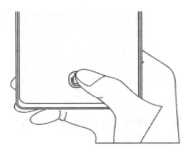

Keep repeating this process until your fingerprint is fully registered and recorded.

5. Once you have finished the registration process for your fingerprints, click on the "Done" button. After selecting the option to check the added fingerprints, you will be able to verify if your fingerprint has been successfully registered.

Unlock the screen with your fingerprint

You can use your fingerprint instead of a PIN, pattern, or password to unlock your screen.

1. Open the Settings app and tap Biometrics & security → and select Fingerprint.

2. Then unlock the screen using the preset screen lock style.

3. Then tap the fingerprint unlock switch to activate it.

4. On the lock screen, place your finger into the fingerprint sensor and scan your fingerprint.

Change the fingerprint icon settings

You can configure your device to show or hide the fingerprint recognition icon if you tap the screen when it's off.

1. Open the Settings app and tap Biometrics & security → Fingerprint.

2. Then unlock the screen using the preset screen lock method.

3. Then tap the Show when screen is off icon and select an option.

Delete your registered fingerprints

Your registered fingerprints can be deleted.

1. Open the Settings app, tap Biometrics & security → then tap Fingerprint.

2. Then unlock the screen using the preset screen lock method.

3. Next, select any fingerprints you want to delete and click Delete.

Face recognition

Your device may be set up to use facial recognition to unlock the screen.

- When you unlock the screen for the first time after turning on the device, you cannot use your face for the screen lock system. You'll need to enter the PIN, pattern, or password you selected when registering your face to unlock your screen so you can use your device. Please be careful not to lose your password, PIN or pattern details.

- If you select the less secure screen lock option "Swipe/None", every piece of your biometric information will be deleted. If you want to use biometric data in apps or other services, you will need to re-register.

Things to note when using face recognition

Before using your device's facial recognition feature, follow these precautions.

- Your device may be unlocked by objects or people that look like your photo.

- Your facial recognition is still less secure than a pattern, password or PIN.

Improve facial recognition capabilities

When using facial recognition, keep the following in mind:

- When registering, please consider these conditions, such as wearing a hat, glasses, mask, heavy makeup, or a beard.

- Make sure your camera lens is clean and you are in a well-lit area.

- Make sure the image is clear for more accurate results.

Register your face

Register your entire face indoors and in the sun to ensure optimal facial registration.

1. Open the Settings app and click the Biometrics & Security → select Face ID.

2. Then read the on-screen instructions and click Next.

3. Then set any screen lock method.

4. You should then position your face within the screen frame. Your camera then scans your face.

•   If your device screen is not working properly using Face Unlock, you can re-register your face by deleting it by tapping "Delete Face Data".

•   To improve facial recognition, select Add alternative appearance to improve recognition, and then add an alternative appearance.

Unlock screen with your facial recognition

You can also use your face to unlock your screen instead of a password, pattern, or PIN.

1. Open the Settings app and tap Biometrics & Security → select Face ID.

2. Then use the preset lock screen method to unlock the screen.

3. Then tap the Face Unlock switch to activate it.

4. Then view the lock screen.

Once your face is recognized, you don't need to use any other screen lock method. If your face isn't shown, use the default lock screen method

Delete your registered facial data

You can choose to delete registered face data.

1. Open the Settings app and tap Biometrics & Security → select Face ID.

2. Then use the preset lock screen method to unlock the screen.

3. Then click "Delete Face Data" → Then click "Delete".

Once your registered face is deleted, all related functions will also be disabled.

Chapter Four
Camera

Introduce

You can capture photos and videos using different modes and settings.

Photo etiquette

- Do not take photos or videos of other people without their consent.

- Please do not take photos or videos in illegal areas

- Do not take photos or videos where they may invade other people's privacy.

Take your photo

1. Open your camera app.

In an alternate approach, you have the option to either drag your app towards the left side of your locked screen or rapidly press your side key twice to swiftly open it.

- When the camera application is opened from the locked screen or when the screen is off with the screen lock method enabled, specific camera features may not be available.

- Your camera will automatically power off when it is not being used.

Depending on your model or service provider, there may be certain methods that are not available to you.

2. To ensure proper focus, simply tap the desired area on your preview screen where your camera should be directed.

To adjust the brightness of the image, simply drag the adjustment bar located above or below the circular frame.

3. Press ◯ to capture an image.

In order to change your shooting mode, simply swipe right or left on your preview screen, or alternatively, drag your finger toward the right or left on your shooting mode menu.

- Preview screens may vary depending on the camera being used and the shooting mode selected.

- When taking high-resolution or zoomed-in photos or videos, it is important to maintain a reasonable distance from your subject in order to ensure clear focus. If you get too close, the clarity of your images or videos may be compromised.

- If your photos appear blurry, attempt to clean the lens of your camera and capture another shot.

- Ensure that your lens is free from any impurities or harm. Failure to do so may result in your device not operating properly in specific modes that require superior image quality.

- The lens on your device's camera is designed to capture wide-angle shots. It's important to note that wide-angle images or videos may exhibit a slight distortion, but this is completely normal and does not indicate any performance problems with your device.

- The maximum recording capacity of a video may vary depending on the resolution you choose.

- When your device experiences a rapid shift in air temperature, it is possible for condensation or fog to develop on your camera. This occurs due to the disparity in temperature between the interior and exterior camera cover. To prevent this, it is important to avoid exposing your camera to such conditions when you plan to use it. In the event that fogging does occur, it is recommended to allow your camera to naturally dry at room temperature before taking photos or recording videos. Failure to do so may result in blurry outcomes.

Settings

Zoom

Recording modes

Gallery

Switch cameras

Capture

Use your camera button

- To initiate the video recording, simply press and hold the camera button.

- To capture burst shots, simply swipe your camera button towards the edge of the screen and keep it pressed.

- To capture more convenient photos, simply rearrange the camera button on your screen by adding an additional one. Access the preview screen and navigate to the ⚙ → Recording methods option. From there, toggle the button for your Floating Shutter to enable it.

Photo mode

To easily capture photos, your camera automatically adjusts recording settings based on your surroundings.

From the list of recording modes, click Photo, then press ◯ Take a photo.

Take your selfie

Take a selfie using the front camera.

1. Swipe up or down on the preview screen or tap 🔄 to switch to the front camera and take a selfie.

2. Then view the front camera footage.

To take a wide-angle selfie of a person or landscape, tap 👥 .

3. Then press ◯ to take a photo.

Apply filters and beauty effects

Before you take a photo, you can simply select any filter effect and adjust your facial features, such as skin tone or face shape.

1.   Click ☀ on the preview screen

2 Select any effect and capture a photo.

Lock focus (AF) and exposure (AE)

To prevent the camera from automatically adjusting based on changes in subject or light source, you can lock focus or exposure to a specific area.

When you tap and hold in the focus area, your focus and exposure settings will be locked and the AF/AE frame will appear in the area. No matter when you take a photo, the lock will stay in place.

Video mode

Your camera adjusts its recording options based on the environment to make the recording video easier.

1.   From the shooting mode menu, tap Video, then tap ⦿ Record video.

•   Tap ⦿ to capture an image from the video while recording.

- Change focus by pressing and holding the point you want to focus on while recording video. To use autofocus mode, you can tap 🔒 to cancel setting focus manually.

2. Click ⏺ to stop recording video.

Portrait mode

Your camera allows you to focus on your subject and take photos clearly with a blurred background.

1. Tap Portrait in the shooting mode menu.

2. Then drag the background blur adjustment bar to adjust the blur level.

3. After "Ready" appears on the preview screen, click ◯ to take a photo.

Background blur adjustment bar ——

- Use this feature in a well-lit area.

49

- Your background blur may not be applied correctly in these situations:
  - If your device or subject is constantly moving.
  - If your subject is very thin or even transparent.
  - If your subject has the same color as the background.
  - If your theme or background is very simple.

Professional grade

Professional mode allows you to manually change various shooting options, such as exposure and ISO value, while capturing an image.

Tap More → and select PRO from the shooting mode menu. To take a photo, select an option, adjust the settings, and tap ◯.

Available options

- ISO: Select any ISO value. It manages the camera's sensitivity to light. Low values are suitable for stationary or well-lit objects. Higher values are suitable for fast-moving or dimly lit objects. However, higher ISO settings may introduce noise in your photos.

- EV: Change your exposure value. This adjusts the amount of light reaching the camera sensor. To compensate for the lack of light, increase the exposure.

- WB: Choose an appropriate white balance to ensure your photo has a true color spectrum. Their color temperature is adjustable.

Separate focus area and exposure area

Your focus area and exposure area can be separated.

Touch and hold the preview screen. Your AF/AE box will appear on the screen.

To separate the focus area from the exposure area, you should drag the frame to the desired location.

Panorama mode

Panorama mode can be used to take multiple photos and then stitch them together to create a vast scene.

1. In the shooting mode menu, tap More → and select Panorama.

2. You can tap ⬭ and move the device slowly in one direction.

Keep the image in your camera's viewfinder. If your preview image exceeds the guide frame or you do not move your device, your device will automatically stop taking pictures.

3. You can tap ⦿ to stop taking pictures.

Avoid taking photos with unclear backgrounds, such as plain walls or empty skies.

Food pattern

Capture food images with more vivid colors.

1. From the shooting mode menu, tap More → Food.

2. Tap the screen, then drag the circular frame across the area to highlight it.

Areas outside the circular frame will be blurred

To adjust the size of your circular frame, simply drag any corner of the frame.

3. Next, you can simply tap 🌡 and drag the adjustment bar to customize and fine-tune the color tone according to your preference.

4. Capture a photo by simply tapping ⭕ on the designated area.

Personalizing the configurations of your camera to suit your preferences

To access additional features on your preview screen, simply tap on ⚙. It's important to note that certain options may not be accessible depending on your chosen shooting mode.

Characteristics of high intelligence

- Enhance your device's capabilities with the scene optimizer feature, which automatically applies an optimal effect tailored to your subject or scene, while also allowing you to customize your color settings.

- To enable QR code scanning, adjust the settings on your device from the preview screen.

Pictures

- By swiping the shutter button, you have the ability to select an action to be performed when you swipe the camera button towards the edge of your screen and hold it.

- When capturing images, it is recommended to utilize the High Efficiency Images Format (HEIF) for optimal picture quality and efficiency.

Selfies

- Customize your device settings to ensure that front-facing camera selfies are saved in their original form as they appear on the preview screen, without any alterations such as cropping or rotation.

Videos

- You have the option to record videos using the High Efficiency Video's Codec (HEVC) format, which allows for reduced file sizes. In order to save storage space on your device, it is recommended to compress your HEVC videos into smaller files.

Sharing HEVC videos online or playing them on different devices is not possible.

General

- Capture your images with vibrant colors and accurately preserve details in both bright and dark conditions with the Auto HDR feature.

- The inclusion of grid lines on the viewfinder serves as a helpful tool for selecting subjects and composing the shot effectively.

- With location tags, you have the ability to attach the GPS coordinates of your current location to any photo you take.

- In certain areas, such as between buildings or in low elevation regions, as well as during unfavorable weather conditions, the strength of your GPS signal may experience a decrease.

- To avoid the possibility of your location being revealed through your uploaded images, it is advisable to disable the location tag settings. By doing so, you can ensure that your images do not inadvertently disclose your whereabouts when shared online.

- When it comes to capturing images or videos, it is advisable to select multiple shooting methods.

- Upon opening your camera, it is possible to save your most recent settings, such as the shooting mode, for future use.

- When selecting a storage location, opt for the memory-based option. The act of inserting a memory card will prompt the availability of this feature.

- To protect your photos, consider adding a watermark to the lower left corner of each image when capturing them.

Privacy

- To access your privacy notice, please click on the provided link.

- Take a moment to review the necessary permissions required for utilizing the Camera application.

- Take the necessary steps to restore your camera's settings to their default state.

- Ensure that you review the legal information and verify the version of your Camera application.

- Please contact us for any inquiries or concerns. You can refer to our FAQ section for commonly asked questions or submit your own inquiries. Additionally, please review our privacy notice for further information.

Depending on the model you have, there may be certain features that are not available for access.

Samsung account

Your Samsung account serves as an integrated account and allows you to use various types of Samsung services available on your smartphone, TV and Samsung website. Go to account.samsung.com to see a list of supported services for your Samsung account.

1. Open the Settings app and tap Samsung Account.

Alternatively, you can open the Settings app and tap "Accounts & Backup" → then "Manage Accounts" → select "Add Account" → then tap "Samsung Account."

2. If you already have a Samsung account, you should log in to your Samsung account.

- If you want to log in with a Google account, click Continue with Google.

- If you do not have a Samsung account, you should click Create Account.

Find ID and reset password

From your Samsung Account login screen, select "Find your ID/Forgot your password?" if you forgot your Samsung Account ID or password. After entering the required information, you can retrieve your ID or change your password.

Sign out of Samsung account

When you log out of your Samsung account, your data, including contacts and events, will be deleted from your mobile device.

1. Open the Settings app, tap Accounts & Backup → and select Manage Account.

2. Then tap Samsung Account → Then select My Profile and tap Sign Out on the bottom screen.

3. Then tap Exit, enter your Samsung account password, and tap OK.

Chapter Five
Enter your text

keyboard layout

As you enter text, your keyboard will appear automatically.

Expand toolbar

Some languages may not allow text input. You must change the input language to another supported language to enter text.

Change your input language

You should click ⚙️→ then select language and type → then click Manage input languages and select the language you want to use. If you select multiple languages, you can switch input languages by swiping left/right using the space bar.

Replace keyboard

Click ⌨️the navigation bar to change keyboards.

To change the keyboard type, tap →, then select Language and type, select any language, and then select the desired keyboard type.

- Open the Settings app, select General Management → Then tap Keyboard List & Defaults, then tap the keyboard button on the navigation bar switch to enable it (if your keyboard button (⌨️) is not visible on the navigation bar.

- On a 3x4 keyboard, a key contains three to four characters. To enter characters, tap the appropriate keys until the desired character appears.

Copy and paste

1. You should click and hold on any text.

2. Then drag or select the desired text. You can even click Select All to select all text.

3. You can then click Copy/Cut.

Carefully selected text will be copied to the clipboard.

4. To paste text, press and hold the desired location and tap "Paste".

To paste previously copied text, press "Clipboard" and select your text.

Install/uninstall applications

Galaxy Store

Download and purchase your app. An application developed specifically for Samsung Galaxy smartphones is available for download.

Open your Galaxy Store app. You can click to search for new keywords or browse apps by category.

-   Availability of this application may vary by model or service provider.

- Tap Menu →⚙→, then select Auto-update apps, select an option, and adjust auto-update settings.

Play Store

Purchase and download the app.

Open your Play Store app. Apps can be found using keyword searches or browsing by category. You can change your auto-update settings if you click the account icon, select Settings → Network settings → Auto-update apps, and then select an option.

Manage your applications

Removing or deactivating applications

To access various options, tap and hold an application of your choice.

- To remove downloaded applications, simply uninstall them from your device.

- Deactivate: By deactivating this option, you can effectively render your pre-installed default applications inoperable. It is important to note that not all applications may be compatible with this feature.

Empowering your software programs

To access your Settings app, simply open it and navigate to the Apps section. From there, select the Disabled option, and confirm by tapping OK. You can then choose any app you desire and enable it by tapping on it.

Establishing the permissions for your application

In order to operate effectively, certain applications may necessitate permission to access or utilize information from your smartphone.

To access your app permissions, navigate to the Settings app and select Apps→⋮→. From there, you can choose a specific app and tap on Permissions to view and modify its permissions. The ability to both view and adjust app permissions is available.

To modify the permission settings for your app, begin by accessing the Settings app on your device. From there, navigate to the Apps section and proceed to the

Permission manager. Within this menu, you will have the ability to adjust your app's permissions based on category. Simply select the desired category and then choose the specific application you wish to modify. In the event that you neglect to grant permissions to applications, the essential functionalities of your applications may experience disruptions in their proper functioning.

Chapter Six
Phone

Introduction

You have the ability to initiate or respond to voice and video calls.

If you find that there are unwanted sounds during a phone call, it could be because the upper microphone is being obstructed. To resolve this issue, remove any accessories, such as stickers or screen protectors, that may be covering the area around the upper microphone.

Engaging in telephone conversations

1. To access the Keypad, open the Phone app and proceed to tap on it.

2. Please input any phone number of your choice.

3. To initiate a voice call, simply tap on the designated button, or alternatively, tap on the corresponding button to initiate a video call.

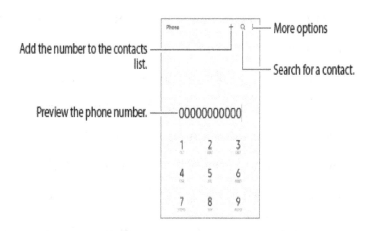

Add the number to the contacts list.

Preview the phone number. ——00000000000

More options

Search for a contact.

Making phone calls directly from your call history or list of contacts

To make a call, start by opening your Phone app, then navigate to the Recents/Contacts section and swipe right on a phone number or contact.

In the event that this function is deactivated, simply tap on ⋮ → the screen and navigate to the Settings menu. From there, select other calls settings and locate the Swipes to call / text toggle to enable it.

Utilizing the convenient feature of speed dialing

To assign a phone number to speed dial, follow these steps: Open your Phone app and navigate to either the Keypads or Contacts→ ⋮ → section. From there, locate the Speed Dials option and select it. Choose any available speed dialing number and proceed to enter the desired phone number. To make a call using speed dial, simply tap and hold the corresponding speed dial number on your keypad. For speed dial numbers 10 and above, tap on the first digit(s) of the number and then tap and hold the final digit.

As an example, in the case of setting up a speed dial number as 123, you would need to press the keys 1 and 2, followed by tapping and holding down the key 3.

Engaging in international phone conversations

1. To access the keypad on your phone, simply open the Phone app and proceed to tap on the Keypad option.

2. To make the plus sign appear, tap and hold the number zero for a few seconds.

3. Please input your country code, phone number, and then proceed by tapping on the designated area.

Receive calls

Responding to incoming phone calls

In the event of a phone call, it is advisable to step outside of your larger social group.

Rejecting calls

Whenever a call comes in, make sure to drag outside of the large circle.

Upon declining an incoming call, you have the option to slide the message delivery bar upwards and select the message you wish to send.

Open the Phone app, tap ⋮→, then select Settings →, then tap Quick reject messages. Enter a message and click ✛ to create a different rejection message.

Block phone number

You can block calls from specific numbers that have been added to the block list.

1. Open your Phone app, tap ⋮→, then select Settings →, then tap Block numbers.

2. Then tap Recent/Contacts, select a phone number or contact, and tap Done. To enter a number manually, click Add phone number, enter the phone number, and click ✝.

You won't receive a notification when a blocked number tries to contact you. All calls will be documented in your call history.

 Calls from people who don't show caller ID may also be blocked. Touch the "Block unknown/private numbers" switch to simply enable this feature.

Contact person

Introduce

You can manage contacts or create new contacts on your mobile device.

Add contacts

Create new contact

1. Open the Contacts app and tap ✝.

2. Select your storage location.

Then enter your contact information and click Save.

Import contacts

You can add contacts to your device by importing them from other storage devices.

1. Open the Contacts app and tap☰ → Select Manage Contacts → Then tap Import/Export Contacts → Then select Import.
2. Go through the on-screen commands to simply import contacts.

Sync your contacts with web accounts

Sync contacts on your device with online contacts stored in a web-based account such as a Samsung account.

1. Open the Settings app, tap Accounts & Backup → select Manage Accounts, then select the account you want to sync.
2. Next, tap "Sync Accounts" and then tap the "Contacts" switch to turn it on.

Search your contacts

Open your Contacts app. Then tap 🔍 at the top of your contact list and enter your search criteria.

Tap your contact. Then do one of the following:

- : Make a voice call.

- / : Make a video call.

- : Compose your message.

- : Compose an email.

Remove your contact

1. Open the Contacts app and tap ⋮ → Select Delete Contact.

2. Select the contact and tap Delete.

To delete contacts individually, select them from the contact list, select More →, and tap Delete.

Share your contacts

You can share your contacts with others by using various sharing options.

1. Open the Contacts app, tap ⋮ →, and select Share Contact.

2. Select a contact and tap Share.

3. Select any sharing method.

Create group

You can manage your contacts through groups and add groups, such as friends or family.

1. Open the Contacts app and tap $\equiv$ → then select Groups → tap Create group.

2. Follow the on-screen instructions to create the group.

Merge duplicate contacts

If your contact list contains duplicate contacts, consider merging these contacts into one to optimize your contact list.

1. Open the Contacts app and tap $\equiv$ → Then select Manage Contacts → Then tap Merge Contacts.

2. Then check your contacts and click Merge.

Message

Introduce

You can send and receive messages based on conversations.

Send Message

1. Open the Messages app and tap.

2. Add recipients and enter your message.

To record and send a voice message, press and hold 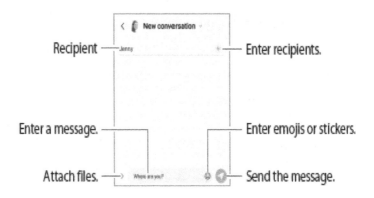, speak your message, then lift your finger. Your recording icon will only appear if there is nothing in your message input field.

3. Then tap to send the message.

Recipient — Jenny — Enter recipients.

Enter a message. — — Enter emojis or stickers.

Attach files. — — Send the message.

View message

1. Start the Messages application and simply click on the Conversations.

2. Select any contact or phone number in the message list.

• To reply to a message, touch the message input field, type your message, and click .

- Pinch or spread two fingertips on the screen to adjust font size.

Sort your messages

Messages can be sorted by categories and easily managed.

Your messages can be sorted by categories and easily managed

Open the Messages app, select Conversations → and click ✛ .

To enable your category options (if they are not visible), click ⁝ Settings, then click Switch Conversation Categories.

Remove message

You must tap and hold on a message before tapping "Delete" to delete it.

Change your messaging settings

Open the Messages app, tap ⁝ →, and select Settings. You can block unwanted messages and even change notification settings and more.

Internet

Use the Internet to search for information and bookmark your favorite websites for easy access.

1. Open your internet application.

2. Then enter any keywords or your URL and click "Start".

Drag your finger slightly down on the screen to display the toolbar.

To swiftly switch between tabs, simply swipe left or right on your address field.

Employ your secret mode

By setting a password for your secret mode, you have the ability to prevent others from accessing your bookmarks, saved pages, search history, and browsing history.

1. To activate Secrets mode, simply tap⬚→ on the "Turn on" option.

2. To activate the Lock Secrets mode, simply tap on the toggle and proceed to tap on Start. From there, you can set up a password for the secret mode.

When your device is in secret mode, the color of the toolbars will be altered. To deactivate secret mode, simply tap on⬚→ choose Turn off Secrets mode.

While in secret mode, the use of specific features, such as screen capture, is restricted.

Samsung's Pay

Introduction

For a seamless and reliable payment experience, easily register your cards with Samsung Pay, enabling you to make swift and secure transactions both online and offline.

- In order to utilize Samsung Pay for transactions, your smartphone may require a connection to either a mobile network or Wi-Fi, depending on your geographical location.

- The presence of this feature may differ depending on the model or service provider you have.

- The steps required for your initial setup and card registration may vary depending on your service provider and model.

Configure your Samsung Pay for optimal usage

When launching this application for the first time or after resetting the data, make sure to follow the on-screen instructions to complete the initial setup process.

1. To begin, access your Samsung Pay application.

2. Once you sign into your Samsung account, carefully review and agree to the terms and conditions as you read through them.

3. To enhance the security of your transactions, it is recommended to establish a personal identification number (PIN) and register your fingerprint for authentication purposes when using Samsung Pay. This PIN will be required to validate various operations within the app, such as bill payments and unlocking the application.

Register cards

To register your card, simply open the Samsung Pay app and carefully follow the on-screen instructions provided.

Engaging in the act of making financial transactions

1. To select a card for use, begin by tapping and holding the card image located at the bottom of your screen. Drag the card image upwards to proceed. Alternatively, you can access your Samsung Pay application. Once opened, swipe

left or right to navigate through your list of cards and choose the one you wish to use.

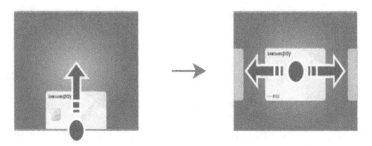

2. To complete your payment, either input the PIN you established or utilize fingerprint scanning.

3. Place the rear of your mobile device against the card reader.

Once your card details are recognized by the card reader, your payment will be promptly processed and executed.

- In the event of network connectivity issues, there is a possibility that payment processing may encounter failures.

- Various payment verification methods may be utilized depending on the type of card readers you have.

Cancel your payments

To cancel your payments, simply visit the location where you initially made them.

In order to select the cards you wish to use, simply swipe right or left on your list of available cards. To complete the cancellation of your payment, follow the instructions displayed on your screen.

Samsung Notes

You can create notes by handwriting, using the keyboard, or drawing on the screen. Images and audio recordings can also be added to your notes.

Create notes

1. Open the Samsung Notes app, then tap ⓔ and create a note.

You can change the input method by clicking ⓐ or ▤

2. After writing your note, click the Back button to save it. To save the note in a different file format, tap → and select Save as file.

Remove note

To delete it simply tap and hold on the note, then tap Delete.

Samsung Health

Introduce

With Samsung Health, you can better manage your fitness and health. Set fitness goals, monitor your progress and log your overall health and fitness. Additionally, you can view health recommendations while comparing the steps in your log with those of other Samsung Health users.

How to use Samsung Health

Open the Samsung Health app. To complete setup, follow the on-screen instructions when using the app for the first time or when restoring after a data reset. To change any item, select Manage items from the main card list at the bottom of the Samsung Health home screen.

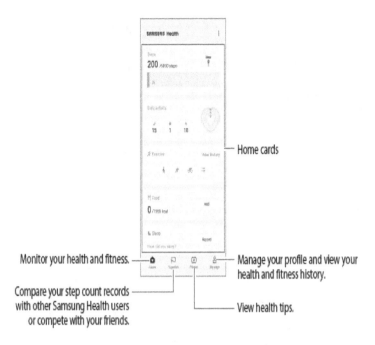

Home cards

Monitor your health and fitness.

Manage your profile and view your health and fitness history.

Compare your step count records with other Samsung Health users or compete with your friends.

View health tips.

- Some features may not be available depending on your location.

- If you use your step card while traveling by train or car, vibration may affect your step count.

Calendar

Keep your schedule in mind by entering upcoming events into your planner.

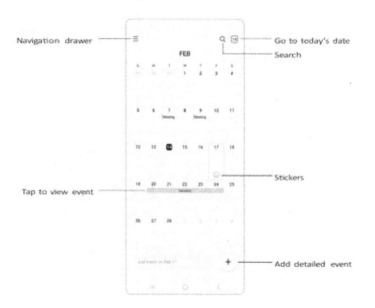

Create event

1. Open the Calendar app and tap ⊕ or double-tap a date.

If you already have a saved task or event for that date, click the date, then click ⊕.

2. Then enter your event details and click Save.

Sync events with your account

1. Open the Settings app, tap Accounts & Backup → select Manage Accounts, then select your sync account.

2. Then click Sync Accounts and then click the Calendar switch to turn it on.

Open your Calendar app and tap → ~→ Select Manage Calendars✛→ Add account for sync. Next, select the account you want to sync and log in. When added, a blue circle will appear next to your account name.

In addition to the accounts you want to sync, carefully open the Calendar app and tap☰→⚙→ Manage Calendars →✛. Then manually select the account you want to sync and log in to.

Once an account is added, a blue circle will appear next to the account name.

Memory

Set conditions for receiving notifications and register for reminder tasks.

- Connect to a cellular or Wi-Fi network for more accurate notifications.

- GPS functionality must be enabled to use your location alerts. Availability of location reminders varies by model.

Start your memory

Open the Calendar app and tap $\equiv \rightarrow$ Select reminder. Your Reminders screen will appear, and your Reminders app icon will be added to your Apps screen.

Create your memories

1. Open your Reminders app.

2. Then click ✚, enter your information, and click Save.

Complete your memories

In the reminder list, click ☐ or select a reminder, then click Done.

Restore your memory

You can resume completed reminders.

1. In the reminder list, select $\equiv\rightarrow$ and click Done.

2. Select any category and tap Edit.

3. Select the memory you want to restore and tap Restore.

Such reminders will be added to your reminder list and you will be reminded again.

Erase your memory

Select the reminder and click Delete to delete it. To delete multiple reminders, press and hold the reminder, highlight the reminders you want to delete, and tap Delete.

Chapter Seven
My Files

You have the ability to conveniently access and organize a diverse range of files that are stored on your device.

Access your My Files application

To free up storage space on your device, simply tap on the "Analyze storage" option to initiate a scan for unnecessary data. Additionally, you can press Q the designated button to search for specific folders or files.

Clock

Open your Clock application to access a range of features. With this application, you can conveniently set the time for an event, check the current time in various cities across the globe, set alarms, or even select a specific time duration.

Calculator

Whether it be simple or complex calculations, you are able to perform them with ease.

Please launch the Calculator application.

- ⏱ : Access your record of calculations. Tap Clear history to erase your calculation history. Tap 🖩 to exit the panel displaying your calculation history.

- 📏 : Utilize your tool for converting units to seamlessly transform various quantities, such as area, length, and temperature, into alternative units.

- 🖩 : Activate the display function on your scientific calculator.

SmartThings

With the use of your smartphone, you have the ability to control and manage your smart appliances and Internet of Things (IoT) devices.

For additional information, access the SmartThings application and navigate to the Menu section where you can find a guide on how to use it.

1. Launch your SmartThings application.

2. Then click on Devices → then choose Adds device or tap +.

3. Select a device then connect to it using your on-screen directions.

- Depending on your shared contents or the type of devices connected, several connection methods may apply.

- The device that you connect might vary based on your region. The features that are available may vary based on your device that is connected.

Please take note that the Samsung's warranty does not cover faults or defects pertaining to connected devices. When errors / defects happen in connected devices, reach out to your device's manufacturer.

Smart View

To view your contents on a larger screen, simply connect your mobile device to a TV or monitor that is capable of screen mirroring.

1. To access the (Smart View) feature, begin by opening your notification panel, followed by swiping down and finally tapping on it.

2. Select the appropriate device to mirror the screen of your device.

The resolution of the video played through Smart View may differ depending on the specific model of your TV.

Share Music
Introduction

If your speaker is already connected to a mobile device via Bluetooth, you can utilize the Music Share feature to share the connection with another person. This allows both you and someone else to enjoy the same song simultaneously through your own Galaxy Buds.

This feature can only be utilized by devices that have the Music Share function enabled.

Share your Bluetooth speaker

With the utilization of your Bluetooth speaker, you have the ability to play music from not only your own mobile device but also from your friend's device.

1. Make sure that you have successfully established a connection between your Bluetooth speaker and smartphone.

2. To activate Music Sharing on your smartphone, access the Settings app, navigate to Connections, tap on Bluetooth→ ⋮, go to Advanced, and finally toggle the switch for Music Share.

By tapping on the Music Share option, you can unlock additional features that allow you to control who has the ability to share your smartphone with you.

3. Select the speaker from the list of available Bluetooth devices on your friend's smartphone.

4. Accept your connection's request on your device.

The speaker that you have will be shared among multiple individuals.

When you switch to using your friend's smartphone for music playback, the music playing on your own smartphone automatically pauses.

How to use your Galaxy Buds to listen to songs with friends

By utilizing the earbuds on your smartphone, both you and your friend can enjoy listening to music together.

Among all the devices available, only the Buds series of Galaxy supports this particular feature.

1. Make sure that all smartphones and pairs of earbuds are properly connected.

2. On your friend's phone, open the Settings app and tap "Connections" → select "Bluetooth" → ⋮ → select "Advanced" and tap your Music Sharing switch to turn it on.

3. Click Share Music to access additional features, such as: B. Decide who can share the device with you.

4. On your mobile device, open the notification panel and tap Media output.

5. Click Music Sharing and select your friend's Buds from the list of discovered devices.

6. You should accept the connection request on your friend's phone.

You can listen to music on two headphones at the same time while playing music on your smartphone.

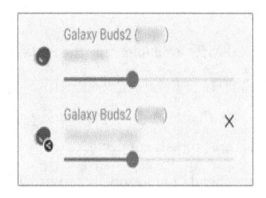

Link to Windows

To instantly access your device's data, including messages or photos, on your Windows PC, simply connect your mobile device to your computer.

You can use your computer to answer calls and messages.

- It is recommended that you use the latest version of Windows and Your Phone app to take full advantage of this feature.

- A Microsoft account is required to access this feature. You can sign in to any Microsoft service or device, including Windows 10 and Microsoft Office, by creating an account.

Connect to your computer

1. Open the Settings application and click the Advanced features → Windows link.

2. Follow the on-screen instructions to connect.

View data and notifications from your device on your computer Open the Phone app on your computer and select the category you want.

Available features and menus may vary by model or software version.

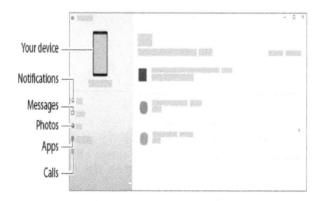

Google apps

Google offers business, social media, and entertainment apps. A Google Account may be required to use some applications.

Please go to each application's Help menu for more information about it.

- Chrome: Use it to browse websites and find information.

- Gmail: Send and receive email using Google's mail service.

- Maps: Use them to see where you are relative to other locations, search global maps, and find your current location.

- YT Music: Enjoy a wide range of music and videos from YouTube Music. You can also listen to and explore your music collection stored on your smartphone.

- Google Play Movies & TV Shows: Get or rent movies and TV shows from the Play Store.

- Drive: Share and store your content in the cloud, accessible from anywhere.

- YouTube: Watch, create and share videos.

- Photos: Search, organize and edit all your photos and videos from multiple sources in one place.

- Google: Quickly search for content using your device or the internet.

- Duo: Make simple video calls.

- Messages: Use your computer or smartphone to send and receive messages and share all types of content, including photos and videos.

Some apps may not be available depending on the model or service provider.

Chapter Eight
Gallery

Introduction

By utilizing the Gallery feature, you have the ability to access and peruse the collection of photos and videos stored on your mobile device. Furthermore, the functionality extends beyond mere viewing, as you can also create captivating stories and efficiently organize your visual content by creating albums.

Make use of your Gallery

Access your Gallery app.

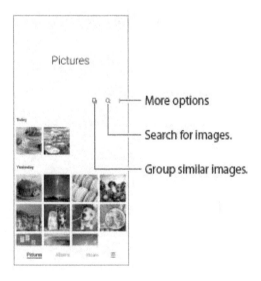

Arranging similar pictures together

To organize and showcase your finest photographs, simply access your Gallery app and select ▢ the option to group similar images. This will allow you to view a preview of your most exceptional shots. If you wish to explore each individual image within the group, simply tap on the corresponding preview.

View your images

Access various files by sliding left or right on your screen after opening the Gallery application and selecting a picture.

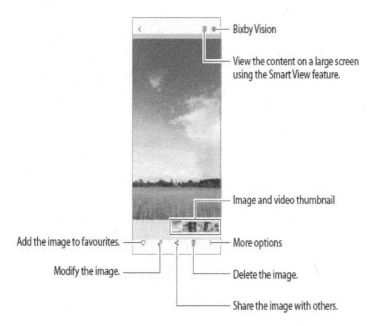

Bixby Vision

View the content on a large screen using the Smart View feature.

Image and video thumbnail

Add the image to favourites.

Modify the image.

More options

Delete the image.

Share the image with others.

Crop your enlarged photos

1. To begin, launch your Gallery application and select any desired image from the available options.

2. Gently separate your index and middle fingers on the desired location before giving it a light tap 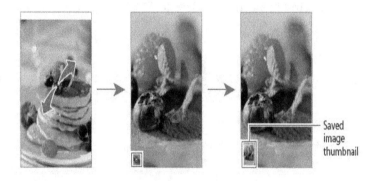 to save.

Once the area is cropped, it will be automatically saved as a file.

Saved image thumbnail

Watch your videos

To initiate the viewing experience, access your Gallery app and select a video of your choice. To explore additional files, simply swipe either to the right or left on your screen.

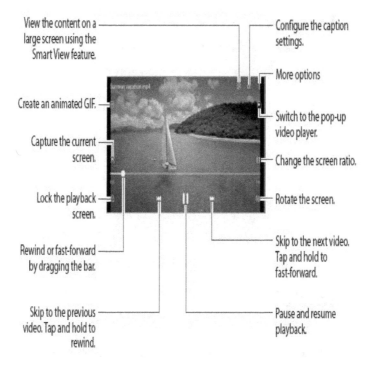

View the content on a large screen using the Smart View feature.

Configure the caption settings.

More options

Create an animated GIF.

Switch to the pop-up video player.

Capture the current screen.

Change the screen ratio.

Lock the playback screen.

Rotate the screen.

Rewind or fast-forward by dragging the bar.

Skip to the next video. Tap and hold to fast-forward.

Skip to the previous video. Tap and hold to rewind.

Pause and resume playback.

To adjust the brightness or volume of the playback, simply swipe your finger up or down on the left or right side of your screen, respectively.

To fast-forward or rewind on your playback screen, simply swipe to the right or left.

Albums

After creating albums, you have the ability to organize your photos and videos accordingly.

1. To create an album, open your Gallery app and navigate to Albums. From there, select the→ ⋮ → option to create a new album.

2. To add your desired pictures or videos, simply select your preferred album, tap on "Add items," and proceed to copy or move them.

Stories

Once you save or capture pictures and videos, your device will automatically process the date and location tags associated with them, subsequently organizing your media and generating captivating stories.

To access your Gallery app, simply open it and then navigate to the Stories section where you can choose from a variety of available options.

In order to include or remove photos and videos, simply select a story and then tap on the ⋮ → option labeled as "Adds" or "Edit".

Synchronizing your collection of photos and videos

To begin the syncing process, open your Gallery application and navigate to the ☰→ Settings→ option. From there, select Sync with OneDrive and carefully follow the on-screen instructions to successfully complete the synchronization. Cloud sync happens with your Gallery app. Once your Gallery app syncs with the cloud, your captured images and videos will be saved in the cloud. You can use the Gallery app and other devices to view videos and images stored in the cloud.

After connecting your Samsung and Microsoft accounts, you can choose Microsoft OneDrive as your cloud storage option.

Remove photos and videos

Open the Gallery app, then tap and hold on an image, video, or story to delete it, then tap Delete.

Use your recycle bin function

You can keep deleted videos and images in Trash. After some time, your files will be deleted.

Open the Gallery app and click ☰→ Select Settings, then tap the Trash button to open it.

To view files in the Trash, open the Gallery app and click ☰→ Trash.

AR Zone

The AR Zone is a designated area for augmented reality experiences.

Introduction

AR Zone is your gateway to all things AR. Take advantage of the various features available and unleash your creativity by capturing captivating images and videos.

Launch your AR Zone

For the launch of AR Zone, you have at your disposal the following methods:

- Access your AR Zone application by opening it.
- To access the AR Zone feature, simply open your Camera app and navigate to MORE, then select AR ZONE.

Depending on your model or service provider, there may be limitations on accessing certain features.

AR Emojis Studio

The AR Emojis Studio is a place where users can create their own personalized augmented reality emojis.

Create your AR Emoji

When it comes to creating emojis, you have the freedom to customize them to your liking, allowing for a fun and enjoyable experience when utilizing their various features.

1. The process of generating AR Emoji involves crafting personalized animated characters.

2. To access AR Emoji Studios, simply open your AR Zone app and tap ⟶ on it.

If you want to make your own emoji, you have the option to select an image or take a selfie.

3. Follow the on-screen instructions to create your own emoji.

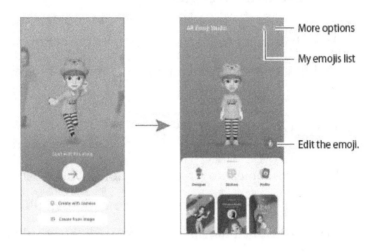

More options

My emojis list

Edit the emoji.

Choosing an AR emoji to utilize

To begin, launch the AR Zone application on your device and navigate to AR Emoji Studios→⚏. From there, you can freely choose any emoji that captures your interest.

Remove AR emoji

Open the AR Zone app, tap AR Emoji Studios→⚏→ 🗑, highlight the emoji you want to delete, and tap Delete.

Create short AR emoji clips and decorate your device with them

You can create a short video using emojis to use as a wallpaper or background image for your calls.

1. Open the AR Zone app and tap AR Expression Studio.

2. Select Create Video, Lock Screen or Call Screen.

3. Then select any template.

To change the wallpaper, tap .

4. Click Save to save your video.

You can view saved videos in the gallery.

5. To use the video directly, you should select an option on the bottom screen.

Create contact profiles using AR emojis

1 Use any emoji in your Contacts app and Samsung account profile picture.

2 Open the AR Zone app and select AR Emoji Studios.

3 Tap Profile and select an emoji.

4 Select the desired pose.

5 Press Done → then Save.

Emoji

Pose

Cancel   Done

AR Sticker Emoji

Create your own stickers by combining emoji expressions and actions. Your emoji stickers can be used on social media platforms or messaging communications.

Create your sticker

1. Open the AR Zone app and tap the AR emoticon sticker.

2. Then tap ╋ at the top of the sticker list.

3. Edit the sticker to your liking, then tap Save.

You can view the stickers you created by clicking "Customize".

Remove AR Sticker Emoji

Open the AR Zone app and tap on the AR Emoji Sticker → ⋮ → and select Delete Sticker. Select the emoji sticker you want to delete and tap Delete.

Use AR stickers in chats

You can use emoji stickers in text messages or social media to join the conversation. The following steps show how to use emoji stickers in the Messages app.

1. While composing a message in the Messages app, tap ☺ Samsung Keyboard.
2. Click on your emoji icon.
3. Select an emoji sticker.

This emoji sticker has been inserted.

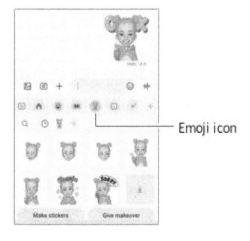

Emoji icon

AR Doodle

Create fun videos by recording doodles or handwriting on faces or other surfaces. When your camera detects a face/room, graffiti on that face moves with the face, while graffiti on the room stays in place regardless of camera movement.

1. Start the AR Zone application and click on the AR Doodle.

When your camera detects your subject, your detection area will appear on the screen.

2. Click 🖊 and write/draw in your recognition area.

- If you have switched to the rear camera, you can also write/draw outside the detection range.

- If you click ⦿ and start doodling, you can also record your own doodling.

110

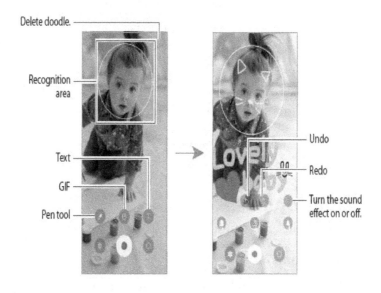

Delete doodle.

Recognition area

Text

GIF

Pen tool

Undo

Redo

Turn the sound effect on or off.

3 Click ⊙ to record video.

4 Click ▣ to stop recording video.

Your videos can be viewed and shared in your gallery.

Depending on the camera you are using, the functionality of the preview screen may vary.

Chapter Nine
Settings

Samsung accounts

To access and oversee your Samsung account, simply log in and navigate to the Settings screen where you can choose the Samsung account option.

Connections

Options

In order to modify your settings for various connections, such as Bluetooth and Wi-Fi, you have the ability to make necessary adjustments.

- To access the Connections menu, navigate to the Settings screen and simply tap on it.

- To connect to a network and access the Internet or other network devices, simply activate the Wi-Fi feature. For more details, refer to the Wi-Fi section.

Bluetooth is a convenient tool for exchanging media files and data between devices that support Bluetooth technology. It allows for seamless sharing and can be easily adjusted alongside other connection settings, such as Wi-Fi.

- To access the Connections feature, simply tap on the Connections option located within the Settings screen.

- You have the ability to set up your device to scan NFC tags, which contain product information. This feature can also be used for contactless payments and buying tickets for transportation or events once you have downloaded the necessary apps. To obtain more information, please refer to NFC and contactless payments (specifically, the models that offer NFC support).

Activate flight mode on your device to disable all wireless connectivity options, leaving only non-network services accessible.

- Always adhere to the guidelines provided by your airline and follow the instructions given by the flight staff. It is essential to ensure that your device remains in-flight mode throughout its usage.

Configure the settings for your mobile network to establish a seamless connection.

- Keep tabs on your data usage and make necessary adjustments to your data limit settings. When you have used up all of your allocated mobile data, set up your device to automatically disable your connection.

- To prevent certain applications running in the background from transmitting or receiving data, you can utilize the data saver feature. For additional information, please refer to the Data saver section.

In addition, you have the option to configure applications to exclusively utilize your mobile data, even if your device is connected to a Wi-Fi network.

- SIM Card Manager: Customize your SIM card settings and activate SIM/USIM cards. For details, see SIM card management.

- Mobile hotspot and tethering: To share your device's mobile data connection with other devices, use it as a mobile hotspot. For more details about hotspots, see Mobile hotspots. If you use this feature, you may need to pay additional fees.

- Additional connection settings: You can personalize settings to control other features.

Wifi

To connect to a Wi-Fi connection and access the Internet or other network devices, turn on the Wi-Fi feature.

Connect to a Wi-Fi network

1. On the Settings screen, tap Connections → select Wi-Fi, then tap the switch to turn it on.

2. Select any network from the list of Wi-Fi networks.

Note that networks with a lock icon will require a password.

- Without a password, your device will automatically reconnect to any Wi-Fi network once connected. To prevent your device from automatically connecting to the network, click the Automatically reconnect switch to turn it off.

- If you are having trouble connecting to the network, try restarting the wireless router or wireless functionality on your device.

View your WiFi network quality information

View quality information about Wi-Fi network speed and stability.

On the Settings screen, tap Connections → Then select Wi-Fi and tap the switch to turn it on. Network quality information appears below your Wi-Fi network. If it is not visible, tap → Advanced and select Show network quality information to enable it.

Can display information about the quality of your Wi-Fi network, such as speed and stability.

Depending on your WiFi network, your quality information may not be displayed.

Share your Wi-Fi network password

You can connect to a secure Wi-Fi connection without entering a password if you ask the person that you're connected to tell you the network password. This feature can only be used between connected devices, and the screen of the other device must be turned on.

1. On the settings screen, tap Connections → select Wi-Fi, then tap the switch to turn it on.

2. Select any network from the list of Wi-Fi networks.

3. Then click Request Password.

4. Accept sharing requests from other devices.

Your WiFi password will be entered into your mobile device and it will connect to your network

Wireless direct connection

Wi-Fi Direct works by connecting devices directly to a Wi-Fi network without the need for an access point.

1. On the settings screen, tap Connections → select Wi-Fi, then tap the switch to turn it on.

2. Then tap → and select Wi-Fi Direct.

Your spotted devices will be registered.

If the device you want to connect with is not listed, make sure to request that the device enables the Wi-Fi Direct feature.

3. Choose one device to establish a connection with.

After receiving approval from the other devices, your devices will establish a connection through Wi-Fi Direct.

From your list, select the device that you wish to disconnect in order to terminate the connection.

Bluetooth

Utilize Bluetooth technology to effortlessly share media files or data with other devices that are Bluetooth-enabled.

- Samsung cannot be held accountable for any loss, unauthorized use, or interception of data transmitted or received via Bluetooth.

- To ensure the security and reliability of data transmission, it is essential to use trustworthy and well-protected devices. It is worth noting that the distance over which data can be effectively transmitted may be reduced if there are any obstacles present between the devices.

- There is a chance that certain devices may not be compatible with yours, especially those that have not undergone testing or received authorization from Bluetooth SIG.

- Avoid using Bluetooth functionality for illegal activities such as file piracy or unauthorized conversation interception for profit. Samsung is not responsible for the consequences of illegal use of the Bluetooth function.

Pair with other Bluetooth devices

1. On the Settings screen, select Connections → then Bluetooth, then tap the switch to turn it on. List these discovered devices.

2. Select the Ant device to pair.

If the device you want to pair with doesn't appear in the list, set the device to enter Bluetooth pairing mode.

While the Bluetooth settings screen remains open, your device will be visible to other devices.

3. To confirm, you should accept the Bluetooth connection request in your device.

Whenever another device acknowledges your Bluetooth connection request, the two devices connect to each other.

To unpair a device, click next to the name of the device you want to unpair, then click Unpair.

Send and receive data

Many applications support Bluetooth data transfer. Data such as contacts and media files can be shared with other devices via Bluetooth. Here are some examples of how to send photos to another device.

1. Start the Gallery application and pick a photo.

2. Then tap ↰ →, then select Bluetooth and select the device to which you want to transfer the images.

If the device you want to pair with doesn't appear in the list, ask the device to turn on the visibility option.

3. You should accept the Bluetooth connection request from the other device.

Chapter Ten
(The NFC-enabled models) NFC & contactless payments

NFC-enabled models have revolutionized the way we make payments, allowing for seamless and convenient contactless transactions.

Your device has an NFC antenna built into it. Be cautious when handling your smartphone to avoid any damage to the NFC antenna.

Access the data stored within NFC tags

By utilizing the NFC feature, you have the ability to access product information directly from NFC tags.

1. To activate NFC and contactless payments, navigate to the Settings screen and tap on Connections, followed by tapping on the switch for NFC & contactless payments.

2. Position your device's NFC antenna near the NFC tag, specifically on the back of your device. This will prompt the display of information retrieved from the tag.

To ensure successful scanning of NFC tags and data retrieval, it is important to verify that your device's screen is both turned on and unlocked. Failure to do so will result in the inability to perform these functions.

Utilizing the NFC functionality to conveniently make payments

To make use of the NFC feature for making payments, it is necessary to enroll in mobile payment services. Contact your service provider to either register or obtain further information regarding this service.

1. To activate NFC & contactless payments, navigate to the Connections section on your Settings screen and toggle the switch accordingly.

2. Place the NFC antenna area of your device against the reader of your NFC card to establish a connection.

3. To configure your default payment application, navigate to the Settings screen, open Connections, select NFC & contactless payments, choose Contactless payments, tap on Payment, and finally select the desired app.

There is a possibility that not all payment apps available will be included in your list of preferred payment services.

Printing

Ensure that the plug-ins for your printer are properly installed on your device. By establishing Wi-Fi or Wi-Fi Direct connections to your printer, you can conveniently print documents and photos directly from your device.

There is a chance that certain printers may not be compatible with your device.

Add printer plug-in

Add a printer plug-in for the printer you want to use with the device.

1. On the settings screen, tap "Connections" → tap "More connection settings" → then select "Print" → tap "Download plug-in".

2. Select and install the printer plug-in.

3. Select the plug-in you installed.

When it comes to printers, your device automatically searches for printers that are connected to the exact same wireless network as it.

4. Then select any printers you want to add.

To add a printer manually, click ⋮ → Select Add Printer.

Print your content

When viewing something, such as an image or document, access the list of options and click Print → Select a printer → All printers... and then click the printer.

Chapter Eleven
Biometrics & security

The field of biometrics and security is closely intertwined, as it involves utilizing unique human characteristics for enhanced protection measures.

Options

You have the ability to modify your device's settings in order to enhance its security measures.

To access the Biometrics & security options, navigate to the Settings screen on your device and tap on it.

- Utilizing face recognition technology, you can conveniently set up your device to unlock the screen by simply using your own face.

- The fingerprint feature allows users to conveniently register their fingerprints in order to unlock their screens.

- Enhanced biometrics settings: This feature allows you to modify your personal preferences regarding your biometric data. Additionally, you have the option to access the version specifically designed for biometric security updates and search for any available updates.

- Google's Play Protect feature enables users to configure their devices to scan for malicious apps and suspicious activities, providing warnings and facilitating the removal of potential threats.

- Stay updated on the latest security measures by checking for software updates and viewing your device's current software version.

- Google Plays system updates provide a convenient way to stay informed about the latest updates and view your current Google Plays system versions.

- Find my phone: You can turn this feature on or off. Visit Samsung's Find My Mobile website (findmymobile.samsung.com) to monitor and manage your stolen or lost device.

- Samsung Pass: Confirm your identity quickly and securely using your biometric data. See Samsung Pass for more details.

- Secure Folders: To protect your applications and confidential content from prying eyes, it helps to create secure folders.

- Private Sharing: Securely share your files with others using blockchain technology.

- Install unknown applications: Configure your device to allow installation of unknown application sources.

- Encrypt/Decrypt SD Card: This sets your device to encrypt files on any memory card.

If you reset your device to factory settings and enable this setup option, your device will no longer be able to read encrypted files. Please do Deactivate this setting before you reset your device.

- Additional security settings: You can configure additional security settings.

Some features may not be available depending on the model or service provider.

Secure folder

Use Secure Folders to protect your sensitive applications and content, including contacts and images, from unwanted access. Even if your smartphone is unlocked, your private apps and content are safe.

Secure Folder acts as the only secure storage area. Data in Secure Folder cannot be shared with other devices through unauthorized means (such as USB/Wi-Fi Direct). Any attempt to change the software or operating system will cause the Secure Folder to automatically lock and become unusable. Make sure to back up a copy of your data to a safe location before saving it to a secure folder.

Set up your secure folder

1. Open the Settings app and tap Biometrics & Security → then select Secure Folder.

2. Then follow the on-screen instructions to complete the setup.

Your Secure Folder screen will appear. The Secure Folder app icon ( ) is then added to your Apps screen.

To change the icon or name of the Secure Folder, click

on ⋮ → and select Customize.

- When you open the Secure Folder application using the default lock style.

- If you lose your Secure Folder unlock code, you can reset it using your Samsung account. To unlock the locked screen, you should tap on the bottom button and enter your Samsung account password.

Configure automatic locking conditions for secure folders

1. Open the Secure Folder app, click ⋮ →, then select Settings →, then tap Auto-Lock Secure Folder.

2. You should then select any option.

To manually lock a protected folder, click ⋮ → and select Lock and exit.

Move your content to a secure folder

You can move content such as videos and images to a secure folder. Follow the steps below to move images from default storage to a secure folder.

1. Open the Secure Folder app, click ⋮ →, and select Add files.

2. Then click "Image", check the image you want to move, and then click "Done".

3. Then click Move.

Your selected items will then be transferred to the secure folder and deleted from the original folder. To copy an item, select Copy.

Depending on the type of content you have, there are different methods for moving it.

Move content from Secure Folder

You can move content from the secure folder to the default storage of the corresponding application. The following steps show an example of moving photos from Secure Folder to default storage.

1. Open the Secure Folder app and tap Gallery.

2. Select any image and click $\vdots$ →, then select Move from Secure Folder.

The items you select will be moved to the gallery in the default storage.

Merge applications

You can add any application for use in Secure Folder.

1. Start the Secure Folder application and click on the ✚.

2. Next, highlight one or more applications installed on the device and click Add.

Delete applications from Secure Folder

To delete an app, press and hold the app and select Uninstall.

Add your account

You should add your Google, Samsung and other accounts. Keep your account in sync with apps in Secure Folder.

1. Open the Secure Folder app and click $\vdots$ → select Settings → tap Manage accounts → and select Add account.

2. Select any account service.

3. Then follow the on-screen instructions to complete account setup.

Hide your secure folder

You can hide the Secure Folder shortcut from the application screen.

Open the Secure Folder app, click ⋮ →, then select Settings and press the Add Secure Folder to Apps screen switch to turn it off.

Or, to disable the feature, open the notification panel, swipe down, and press (Secure Folder). If (Secure Folder) doesn't appear in the Quick Panel, click and drag to add it.

To restore the visibility of Secure Folder, open the Settings app, select "Biometrics & Security" → then tap "Secure Folder" and enable it by clicking the "Add Secure Folder to Apps screen" switch It clicks "Add".

Alternatively launch the notification panel, swipe down, and select (Secure Folder) to disable the feature. If you can't find (Secure Folder) in the

Quick Panel, click ⬤ and drag the button above to add it.

To view Secure Folder again, launch the Settings app, tap Biometrics & Security → Secure Folder, and tap the Add Secure Folder to Apps screen switch to turn it on.

Unmount your secure folder

You can uninstall Secure Folder, its contents and applications.

Open the Secure Folder app and choose ⦂ → Then tap Settings → Then select Additional Settings → Then tap Uninstall.

Create a backup copy of the contents of Secure Folder before unmounting it. Do check your "Move media files from Secure Folder" and then you can easily choose "Uninstall". To view the data backed up to Secure Folder, open the My Files app, select Internal Storage → then select Downloads → and tap Secure Folder.

Privacy

Protect your privacy by changing your setting.

Click Privacy on your device screen.

- Permissions used in the past 24 hours: Permissions that allow you to view feature or application usage history.

- Permission Manager: Helps you view a list of features and applications that have appropriate permissions for use. Your permission settings can also be edited.

- Controls and alerts: This helps you set settings for accessing applications.

- Samsung: Enables you to manage personal information associated with your Samsung account and change your customized service settings.

- Google: This configures your advanced privacy settings.

Some features may not be available depending on the model or service provider.

Place

You can change your permission location settings.

On the Settings screen, click Location.

- Application Permissions: This helps you view a list of apps that have access to your device's location and then edit your permission settings.

- Location Services: View the location-based services your device is currently using.

- Current Access: You can see which apps require your current location.

Chapter Twelve
Digital Wellbeing & parental controls

Parental controls and Digital Wellbeing go hand in hand to ensure a safe and healthy digital environment for children.

Utilize the features of your smartphone to prevent it from encroaching on your daily life by reviewing its past usage history. Additionally, take the opportunity to monitor your children's online activities and establish parental controls for their protection.

To access the Digital Wellbeing & parental control feature, navigate to the Settings screen and simply tap on it.

- Set daily usage goals for your smartphone to manage your screen time effectively.

- Limit app usage with app timers: Utilize timers to control the amount of time you dedicate to each app on a daily basis. Once you exceed the set limit, the software will automatically deactivate and become inaccessible.

- Activate focus mode to maintain your focus on objectives and eliminate any distractions on your device. While in focus mode, you can still utilize the apps that you have authorized for use.

- Activate the bedtime mode to reduce eye strain before going to sleep and prevent any disturbances to your sleep cycle.

- To protect your hearing, ensure that your volume monitor is activated.

- Activate your driving monitor to accurately track the duration of device usage while driving.

- Take charge of your children's digital activities by utilizing parental controls.

Chapter Thirteen
Battery & device care

Introduction

The device care feature provides an assessment of your device's battery life, storage capacity, memory, and system security. By simply tapping your finger, you can also enable automatic optimization for your device.

Maximize the performance of your device

Navigate to the Settings screen and choose Battery & device care. From there, you can tap on Optimize now to initiate the process.

To improve the performance of the device, the quick optimization feature implements the following activities.

- The closure of background applications is necessary to ensure optimal system performance.

- Efficiently handling excessive battery consumption.

- We will conduct a thorough scan to detect any crashed applications and identify any potential malware present on your system.

Utilizing the auto-optimization feature

You have the choice to enable automatic optimization for your device whenever it is not in use.

To activate the auto optimization feature, follow these steps: tap on the arrow icon, then select Automation. Once in the Automation menu, tap on "Auto optimizes daily" and toggle the switch to activate it.

Battery

To ensure how much power is left in your battery and the duration you can use your device, it is important to verify these two factors. If your battery level is low, you have the option to preserve battery power by enabling the energy-saving functionalities. To access this feature, navigate to the Battery & device care section in your Settings menu and then select Battery.

- To extend the battery's lifespan, activate the power-saving mode in order to conserve power.

- You can establish battery usage limits for apps that are not frequently used, ensuring efficient background usage.

- Discover additional options for your battery's configurations by accessing the advanced settings.

The remaining duration of your battery usage is an indicator of how much time you have left before it depletes completely. It's important to note that the actual length of time may differ depending on the specific conditions and settings of your device.

- Power-saving mode may not always provide notifications for certain applications.

You can enable power saving mode to extend battery life.

Storage

You can observe or check the status of used and obtainable memory.

On the Settings screen, select Battery & device care → then tap Storage. Select a category and uninstall apps or delete files you no longer need. Next, select the item or press and then click Delete/Uninstall.

Always observe the status of used and available storage.

- Your operating system and default applications consume internal storage, so actual available capacity is less than advertised.

When you update your device, your available capacity may not remain the same.

- You can check the available capacity of internal storage in the specifications section of Samsung's website.

Memory

On the Settings screen, select Battery & device care →
then tap Storage.

Stop using apps in the background and speed up your
smartphone. Check each app on the list and select
Clean Now.

Device protection

Safeguarding your device from potential harm and
damage.

By utilizing this feature, you have the ability to assess
the security status of your device and conduct a
thorough scan for any potential malware present.

Navigate to the Battery & device care option in your
Settings screen, followed by selecting Device
protection, and finally, initiate a phone scan by
tapping on Scan phone.

The phone's information

You can obtain all the necessary info directly from your Smartphone.

Access the "About phone" option within the Settings menu on your device.

To modify the name of your device, simply tap on the Edit option.

- Gain access to a variety of device information, such as your serial number, WiFi MAC addresses, and the status of your SIM card.

- Gain access to important legal information pertaining to your device, such as your open-source license and safety data.

- You can easily retrieve information about your device's software, such as the firmware and operating system versions it is running.

- Battery details: Monitor the status and obtain information about your device's battery. Gain access to comprehensive details about your device's battery.

www.ingramcontent.com/pod-product-compliance
Lightning Source LLC
LaVergne TN
LVHW051244050326
832903LV00028B/2565